How Ducklings Grow

In memory of Nana, who loved ducks
—D.M.

To my son, Brian,
who has a special love for little creatures
—D.K.

ISBN 0-590-45201-0

Text copyright © 1993 by Diane Molleson.
Illustrations copyright © 1993 by Dwight R. Kuhn.
All rights reserved. Published by Scholastic Inc.
CARTWHEEL BOOKS is a trademark of Scholastic Inc.

12 11 10 9 8 7 6 5 4 3   3 4 5 6 7/9

Printed in the U.S.A.   24

First Scholastic printing, February 1993

How Ducklings Grow

By Diane Molleson · Photographs by Dwight Kuhn

Cartwheel
·B·O·O·K·S·™

SCHOLASTIC INC.

New York   Toronto   London   Auckland   Sydney

It is spring. This mother duck is
looking for a safe place to lay her eggs.

The mother builds a nest
in a clump of grass near the water.
She makes the nest from grass, bits of
dry leaves, and her own feathers.

The mother duck
is called a hen.
She is smaller
than the
father duck.

The father duck
is called a drake.
He has a curl
at the tip
of his tail.

After the hen builds her nest,
she sits on the eggs to keep them warm.
The feathers, leaves, and grass help to
keep the eggs warm, too.

A baby duck
is growing
inside each egg.
All the food
a duckling needs
until it hatches
is inside the egg.

The ducklings get their nourishment from the yolk
— the yellow part of the egg.
In about thirty days, the egg yolks are gone.
The ducklings are now big enough to hatch.

When a baby duck is ready to hatch,
it twists and turns inside the shell.
The eggshell cracks.

On the baby duck's bill is a tiny tooth.
It is called the *egg tooth*.
The duckling uses this tooth to
break through the eggshell.

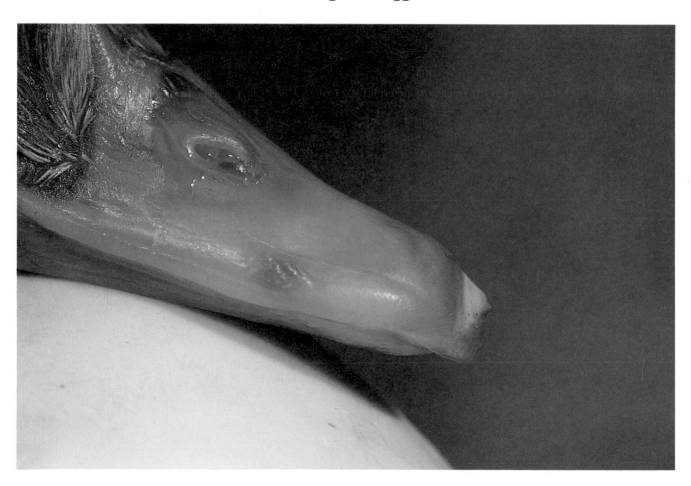

First the duckling scrapes its tooth
against the crack.
That makes the crack grow bigger and bigger.

When the crack is big enough,
the baby duck wiggles through the shell.
Within a day, all the ducklings
in the nest have hatched.
The duckling's egg tooth will fall off
a few days after the duckling has hatched.

Here are the ducklings that were inside the eggs.
They are less than one day old.
The little ducks have wet, sticky feathers.
Their eyes are wide open.

By the next day, the ducklings are dry.
Their feathers are fluffy and soft.
These feathers are called *down*.

Already the ducklings can see and walk.

Just after they hatch, ducklings act as if any large, moving object nearby is their parent.

Sometimes a duckling
will mistake a person,
a chicken,
or even a balloon,
for its parent.

The first large moving object *these*
ducklings see is their real mother.
They follow her out of the nest.
All in a row, they waddle to the water.

The ducklings know how to swim right away.
Nobody has to teach them.

Ducklings are born
knowing everything
they need to live.
They can run,
find food,
and swim.

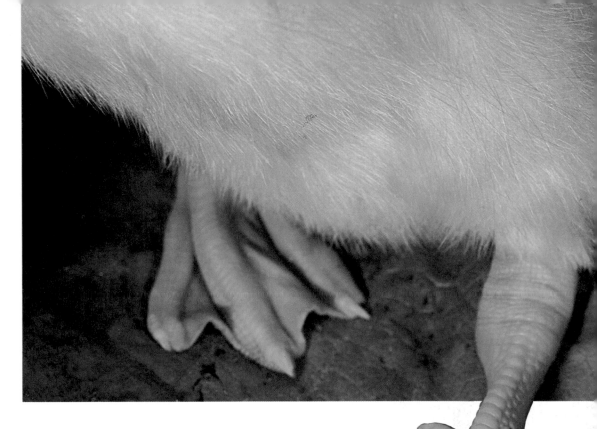

Ducks have webbed feet to help them swim.
These webbed feet work like paddles
in the water.

It is easier for the ducklings to swim
with their webbed feet
than to walk on land.

The ducklings line up behind their mother in the water.

They are off to look for food.

They eat snails, seeds, and small insects,
which they can find on or just under the water.
To get their food, the ducklings tip their tails
up and stretch their necks down into the water.

The ducklings may have trouble
catching a meal when they are very young.
At first they eat mostly snails because baby ducks
are not fast enough to catch insects.

But the ducklings keep trying.

Ducklings take good care of their feathers.
They have a special gland filled with oil
at the base of their tails.
With their beaks, they take the oil
and spread it over their feathers.

Because oil and water do not mix,
drops of water slide right off
this duckling's feathers.

The mother tries to keep her ducklings together.
This way, she can protect them from
snapping turtles, raccoons, and large fish
that want to eat the little ducks.

By the time ducklings are six months old, they are all grown up.
These young ducks have their flying feathers.
They are as big as their parents.
They do not need their mother to take care of them anymore.

This duck flaps its wings and lifts itself
into the air.

By next spring,
when she is
one year old,
this female duck
will be ready
to have ducklings
of her own.

She will try
to find a good
nesting place
in a clump of
grass near
the water.